ALIBI SCHOOL

also by Jeffrey McDaniel

The Forgiveness Parade

The Splinter Factory

ALIBI SCHOOL

Jeffrey McDaniel

manic d press
san francisco

 Published by Manic D Press. For information, address Manic D Press, Box 410804, San Francisco, CA 94141.
www.manicdpress.com

Printed in Canada

Cover art by Slatoff + Cohen

Earlier versions of some of these poems originally appeared in *Casanova, Clockwatch Review, Emeralds in the Ash, Epoch, Exquisite Corpse, Fine Madness, Hammers, Hyper Age, Midland Review, Mudfish, Negative Capability, Nexus, the Pennsylvania Review, Phoebe, Ploughshares, The Rag, Scene, Signs of Life, the Washington Times,* and *Willow Springs*. "Following Her To Sleep" appears in *Best American Poetry 1994.*

Library of Congress Cataloging-in-Publication Data

McDaniel, Jeffrey, 1967-
Alibi school / Jeffrey McDaniel.
p. cm.
ISBN 0-916397-38-6 (pbk.)
I. Title.
PS3563.C3537A79 1995
811'.54--dc20 95-2002
CIP

CONTENTS

THREE

FOUR

ALIBI SCHOOL

Founded in memory of H.C. McDaniel

Between this right world and this wrong world, I refuse to choose.

—Albert Camus

ONE

DISASTEROLOGY

The Badger is the thirteenth astrological sign.
My sign. The one the other signs evicted: unanimously.

So what?! Think I want to read about my future
in the newspaper next to the comics?

My third grade teacher told me I had no future.
I run through snow and turn around
just to make sure I've got a past.

My life's a chandelier dropped from an airplane.
I graduated first in my class from alibi school.

There ought to be a healthy family cage at the zoo,
or an open field, where I can lose my mother
as many times as I need.

When I get bored, I call the cops, tell them
There's a pervert peeking in my window!
then I slip on a flimsy nightgown, go outside,
press my face against the glass and wait...

This makes me proud to be an American

where drunk drivers ought to wear necklaces
made from the spines of children they've run over.

I remember my face being invented
through a windshield.

All the wounds stitched with horsehair
So the scars galloped across my forehead.

I remember the hymns cherubs sang
in my bloodstream. The way even my shadow ached
when the chubby infants stopped.

I remember wishing I could be boiled like water
and made pure again. Desire
so real it could be outlined in chalk.

My eyes were the color of palm trees
in a hurricane. I'd wake up
and my id would start the day without me.

Somewhere a junkie fixes the hole in his arm
and a racing car zips around my halo.

A good God is hard to find.

Each morning I look in the mirror
and say *promise me something*
don't do the things I've done.

THE OFFER

I want to locate a bit of you, cradle it,
say: this, there is no word for this.

But they will. They who name everything
will define our actions
as we auction our bodies off to sleep.

In our single dream we'd compose
a manifesto on the irregularity of scars.

The very idea demands preparation, as if
choosing a school for an angel.

There are no angels. Just those things
blinking like the teeth of jackals
around the moon's significant tremble.

Isolate the idea of shaking our bodies
under the blank comfort of down and tell me
which way will our knuckles face?

Now shake the idea of our isolated bodies
as the sheets become our Miro.

If you stay, the walls will admit their cracks.
See it forming, already on their lips.

THE MULTIPLE FLOOR

Christmas. Again I desert my younger brothers
with freaks disguised as our parents
yanking them back and forth in the snow.

I won't unwrap anyone's expensive feelings for me.
My darkest thoughts dangle from my ears.

An oxygen mask is an abandoned building
neighborhood children learn to breathe in.

A suitcase is what a father carries down
the staircase of broken plates.

I walk through Manhattan, following the footsteps
of God running out on the world.

On Houston Street, a person rattles in a box
like a present so horrible even the wind won't open it.

Glorious and *getting worse* sound the same to me.

Innocence is a finger coming off
in a glove during a snowball fight.

In Tompkins Square, a fiend ties his arm
with Christmas lights and plugs in his only tree.

Panic spreads its hideous cream over the cheeks
of a statue, and I used to be that statue.

I hoist a pale vowel up the throat's pole,
wave it in surrender over the body.

FRIENDS AND HIGH PLACES

for Mike

It's like escaping a hot, bright room
for the serenity of a city at night, covered in snow.

People eliminated. A carpet of silence
for taxis to whisper across. The world becoming

a pleasant dream of itself. The itch
of want smoldering to life on skin. Memory sends

a chill vanishing between vertebrae.
It's New Year's Eve. *Hail the Calendar!* As if

clocks will pause for a moment
before reloading their long rifles. Years are tiny

freckles on the face of a century.
Where is the constellation we gazed at each night

through a bill rolled so tight
the first President lost his breath, as our eyeballs

literally unraveled? I am alone
in the rectangular borough in the observatory,

where even fire trucks can't rescue
the arsonist stretching his calves in my brain.

ALIBI SCHOOL

My pal, Jake, majored in corruption.
His final exam: a girl from the Midwest,

three weeks to dismantle eighteen years
of good parenting. High results came early

in the easy days, with the principal taking
his puff from the honor roll in the bathroom.

In gym we learned how to turn our backs
on the whole world at once; the team

elected me captain of varsity nosebleeds.
At the prom, we parked our limousine

before doing the mandatory wind sprints;
my date's eyes were big, hazel dictionaries.

At our homecoming Jake injected the clouds
with a hero's last breath; rain on the victory parade

was greeted with cheers. The years rushed by
with their tongues hanging out. We packed

our cages and invented course work overseas.
In Guatemala, we copied back pain

for a hundred milligrams of extra credit
and proudly parachuted into sleep. In Prague

we emptied our text books and guzzled
chapters of Bohemian history. The class

kept shrinking until it was just me, passing
all the social tests. I returned to America

fluent in disaster; all the smiles I looked at
collapsed. I walked my pneumonia

up Avenue A, where inconspicuous teachers
assigned telepathic equations. My pupils

leapt from dilated chalkboards; a hundred
consecutive nights of slow, dirty arithmetic

curdled inside of me. Graduation
is an impossibility. Ditto expulsion.

I am permanently unrolled in the rambling
lectures of insomnia. Wake in the lab

with my back against the wall. Turn: the wall
turns with me. I am the mutual friend

of enemy foxholes. It's like bowling
for hostages: exactly beyond my periphery.

THE BOY INSIDE THE TURTLE

Yesterday was an extra-long day
for the boy with no arms
or legs. Neighborhood children
played outside his window.

A soft machine, they circled,
joined hands, closed eyes,
jumped up and down: shoelaces,
giggles moving in time.

One caught the boy peering.
The boy contorted out of sight,
his breaths lumped on one another
like cows in a meat house.

He twisted too slow. *Look,*
it's the turtle! The children
gasped like an audience
responding to a laugh sign.

He shifted his weight left to right,
back left, again right,
then fell from his chair–a pilot
bailing out of a crashing plane.

He was familiar with this
falling. So was his mother.
She'd surrounded his chair
with six layers of towels.

He waited there like a spilled bucket
of green paint. When he no longer heard
any semblance of playing,
he called his mom for help.

TRUE STORY

The main ballroom was packed with the region's elite.
The big band played up a rainbow.
It was our first date, and she was beautiful on the sofa.
My advances were the only thing on the oak table between us.
Even ex-Mayor Cransom threw down his cane and danced
like a cash register before Christmas.
I knew by the way she glanced at my advances
she wanted to wake up next to them.
I leaned forward to drape them around her neck
when a steel beam fell and nearly took off my nose.
My advances weren't as fortunate,
barely breathing beneath a great weight.
All three skywalks in the atrium had collapsed.
Entire families sang under girders.
The floor began to flood.
They had trouble hitting the high notes of optimism.
Rescuers came with chainsaws and torches.
With a forklift they pried the weight off my advances.
The bellhop helped me lift them onto a dolly.
The operator ignored his pain and hailed me a cab.
I threw out the key to room 264.
My advances moaned the whole ride home.
They reeked of booze and cigarettes.
I took off their boots and gave them a bath.

Kansas City, 1987

TECHNOLOGY

The sink's dishes are the sink's problem
as I *ooh* and *aah* at the complexity of balance
implicit to keep the structure: eight glasses, thirteen
bowls, a valley of forks, intact, while I run
hot water over a knife for my onion.

There's a science to the bathtub's archipelago
of grunge colonies that's necessary to America.
My toothbrush is the pin keeping Detroit from collapse.
No, I can't cut my fingernails and risk
re-ordering the universe's distribution of atoms, mass,
stars popping like light bulbs.

And this new, improved imaginary lover–her whiplash
parabola of tongue snaps sandpaper over spine. Yeah,
in thirteen seconds of pure logic I boomerang
to the future and return as a glimpse.

MODERN DAY SISYPHUS

I've fallen down the finest steps in Europe.
Mayan temples in Guatemalan jungle.
The ones Rocky conquered.

It made the flags in my head stop burning.
I grew new flags. Truth is

I had trouble sleeping in the real world.

My social life began to revolve around staircases.
Only went to parties in tall buildings. Yeah,

she's whipped cream looking, an alabaster
personality, but what about her stairs?

Got a flat in an eight-story walkup.
Landings so filthy even the rats turned back.

If you see me between flights, clutching a banister,
don't stare. I'm just a shadow of the mood
swinging inside you.

TWENTYNOTHING

Most kids my age slack on their ass. Not me.
I begin each day with a little project.

Today, I'm gonna give myself a black eye
in every family photograph.

My loony grandmother's coming to visit.
She's got big holes in her mind.

There I am in your backyard, Grandma, right after
you cracked me in the face with the end of a rake.

All I wanted was a Pepsi.
I can't believe you don't remember.

Here I go at my seventh birthday party, when
you knocked some sense into me with a frying pan.

You were drunk. When you sang happy birthday
you referred to me as the mistake. I'll never forget that.

Don't cry, Grandma. I forgive you. For a hundred bucks.
When my father gets home, I'll tell him: *she did it.*

Dad, she went through every family photo album
with a black pen and drew tiny bruises beneath my eyes.

Only your credit card can alleviate the pain.
I'll never make as much money as him.

I'm twentynothing–the distance between a headline
and where our heroes explode,

twentynothing–the time it takes to slide a condom
over the barrel of a handgun,

twentynothing–the remainder of television
over phone sex multiplied by divorce,

twentynothing–the chances of a snowball surviving
the inevitable nuclear hell,

twentynothing–the number of syllables
in the word: disease,

twentynothing–the grimace the brain makes
when confronted with our crater in history.

I'm not lazy like most punks my age,
and I've got a diary to prove it.

Monday: scheduled root canal surgery with every dentist
in San Francisco, which isn't even my time zone.

Tuesday: mailed bomb threats to every Denny's
in America–switch to Dr. Pepper by sunset or else!

Wednesday: sat on my rooftop with a shotgun
and pulverized faxes zipping in from Europe.

Thursday: belched in the face of a smiling
toll booth lady for good luck.

I'm a religious guy. Like Benjamin Péret says
if I see a priest being beaten, I make a wish.

Since orgasm is a prayer reduced to its simplest
expression, I consider myself deeply spiritual.

Recently I had a transcendental experience.
It was like *uuugghh,* with a British accent.

DUTY

Duty calls collect from the alphabet
streets, desolate as Russian vowels.

Gravel pirouettes in his throat: come
now. His pockets bulge with the usual

consonants. Wherever we sit
is a balcony reserved for idiots.

Mourners of clay pigeons, we salute
and nod. The sudden romance

of learning to spell our names
in the emergency of Alphabet City.

We need not look back to confirm–
our footprints glitter along the avenue.

Those who track us will find nilch.
Here comes Dawn with her broom.

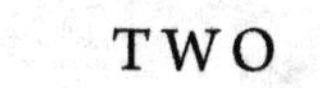
TWO

ANTI-SUICIDE JEWELRY

Wandering through the woods of your absence
I come across a tree, symbolizing
your sexuality and spiritual sanctum.

It is shaped like the Y-vein in your forehead
which I wanted to solve for,
yank like a wishbone,
or spin like a needle to guide me.

I remember discovering you on a bar's peninsula
and immediately surrounding your natives.
You were drinking my logic.
We swallowed the same blueprints.

Your tongue unlocked the swirling keyhole of my ear
as you whispered: *yes*, again and again, so soft
I couldn't hear what you said

except your *S*'es stretched like tendons
over the valley of infants we balanced our piano above.

But I'm not in the vicinity of your falsetto
and the only sound reaching out to me
is the hand of a clock, cracking its sixty knuckles.

JUNCTURE

Action is the shadow of thought. Don't rush me–
the idea I once swore by
was executed publicly at noon.

I feel safe with you. Can you trust me?
Your laugh sticks in my head and your long legs

poke out of my periphery. I don't love you. Did I ever?

Yeah, I admired you across a busy highway, imagined
us scurrying cat-like through the traffic, embracing
on that slab of concrete in the middle.

Our bellies together sounded like a mermaid
banging her tail
against the side of a fish tank.

Our bodies shook like crucial details
in a murder case.

It's only logical–when you kiss reason goodbye
a bruise will prove its purple
theorem on your lip.

That's what I get for serving champagne to an urge.

I undermine your undermine
and backstab your backstab.

In our seamless alibis, we were monsters
and perfect. Now, we're just human.

The sin and repent cycle doesn't run like it once did.

What world have we come to?

THE UNSPOKEN

for Mannal

Five times each day I confess to my image of you,
Try to explain two *k*-sounding *q*'s in Albuquerque,
A series of *u*'s curved like tubs.

Your adobe palms are softer than turquoise.
My fingers the first non-Muslim to swim there.

I believe if one looked in your ear one would see sky:
An intelligent, lobe-bounded blue with languid peacocks
And one cloud so compact it could be chiseled nightly.

You share half a syllable with Albuquerque.
We can't even sit together.

My lone release from pedestal arrest is conversation.
I approach... apoplexy
In the larynx. Lug-worm for a tongue.

I open my mouth to say–
My words are projected between heavens.

OUR SHADOWS DANCE IN RIOT GEAR

She appears like adrenaline.
The wind hums our Byzantine chant.

She glances and all the churches collapse–
dazzling my bonfire into being.

A holy war rages in the throat of her family
where I am the equivalent of pork.

An arrow dipped in her skull's curry whizzes by me.
The exploding plane of marriage is being arranged.

Her terrorist-burgundy lipstick ignites
a rib of dynamite in my mouth's bone fence.

Her fingers will never dig into me like quotation marks
blazing my limbs into parts of speech.

Orangish rumors streak through the junipers.
Our shadows dance in riot gear.

Paralyzed from the thoughts down
I can still wiggle my fantasies.

Her lips are as thick as the skull of a priest.
I will never be Muslim. The sky's one cloud faints.

Our moment expires and two workers
drag it away on a stretcher.

Even this page will have to be burned. Let this sentence
be the arm I can't wrap around her, as she runs up

my phone bill with collect calls from the unconscious.
Somewhere a tidal wave holds still for us.

Sunday is a place that isn't open on Sundays
where I rearrange the stars until she believes me.

AMNESTY

What are my choices
now that I've walked
through the forest
and reached the fence
where the world ends
I emptied my pockets
long ago   The trees
have closed behind me
Stars say their prayers
elsewhere   My escort
the badger has turned
into water   Each leaf
contains a photograph
of a Muslim woman
so azure and fluid
wind drops her basket
of thunderclouds
and forgives me

D

When the sun was a child's breath above the Earth
you were the one I turned to
wearing something dark and celestial
like the sky over Colorado.

You were elegant, like a nightstick
balanced on the tip of a steeple

and seductive, like watching an archer
untie her bow.

You were the one I trotted back to, like a horse
with a bell around my neck
and dangerous, like polishing the horn of a ram.

You rendered me crazy, like the footprints
of a husband chasing his wife
with a garage door opener through the snow.

You were mysterious, like a chandelier
suspended by a rattlesnake.

Your palms were the islands
of sleep I swam between.

A kiss with you was like driving off a cliff
clutching a sawed-off telescope.

When I split, pain spread through the rumor
of my body like truth.

Knees turned to powder in their caps.

I rolled back and forth on the floor
like a four-syllable word.

Every child I looked at
began coughing uncontrollably.

Every building I entered
became the house of separate beds.

Here is a bag filled with the vowels
that tumbled out of me.

Here is the sand castle I destroyed
with the limb of a friend.

Here is the sound of a hero
outgrowing his confetti.

Here, where the stars are scraps of metal
holding the world in place.

FIRST PERSON OMNISCIENT

I made her tell me of the affair,
    every detail,
and I became him, the man who pulled
    her into the closet,
opening the many rooms of her mouth,
    knobs spinning,
and then I was her, pulling him
    by the tongue
through the river of rooms in the mansion
    of my mouth,
his eye pressing into me, his eye
    seeing all,
and then I was the closet, the space
    they traveled through
on their way to the mansion, and then the real
    I entered the closet,
the wind of doors slamming, bodies
    rushing, gone–
my eye lost in the mouth of my pocket,
    or is it my hand,
my dirty, awful hand.

FOLLOWING HER TO SLEEP

My friend wears boots to sleep
so I might learn her path.
I know the way now.

The room is as silent as a child in a closet.

I hang this notion from an instrument of hindsight
where it rocks at the appropriate moments like fortune's
cube on a string.

My neighbor with no arms wanted to know how it feels
to let something go.

I will need more than this map to get to sleep.

I tend the jonquils emerging from the volcanic
soil of her scalp.

A wave repeats itself in a birdcage.

I pay an elderly man to sit in a booth
and keep track of what crosses my mind:
a wedding where the only guests are former lovers
arranged by breast and penis size,
a doctor committing an emergency,
the echo of a silent *e*,
a plane always on the verge of landing.

Morale is down in the boneless,
lactic fist of my genitals.

I cut my fingernails and glue them inside a diary
under the heading: definitive text.

Once I slept like a staircase in an abandoned home.
Now the shape of the body and the body
compete for the same seat.

Make each person's nose the size of their ignorance.

I am irresponsible. I lose the stars off my flag
which is invalid.

Tum on the lights and go to bed!

Check the bags under my eyes for explosives.

I sleep in separate beds.

TRUST

Who do I believe
now that the footprints
have been spun to face
one another–here
where night comes
and disassembles
her outfit of stars?

JUSTICE

for Ivy

Under the gathered hiss of double surveillance
Julius and Ethel Rosenberg meet for the last time.

His fingers, the color of bananas crated in a box,
extend. His palm, open as the white walls

they wake to, closes around her wedding ring
finger. Her hair is as curly as the handcuffs

forcing his right hand to follow the left
in cupping her finger, like a strip of water,

to his lips. His tongue, warmer than the hot water
of Sing Sing, snaps its last glint of salt from her flesh.

Her eyes are the blue of any color skin lathered in ice
and the black of a coal-mining shaft,

where four minutes of darkness make madness
mushroom on a worker's face. Like lasers,

only more complicated, a current ricochets
between their pupils. Tomorrow Joseph

Francel will put his electrician's degree to use, flick
a switch, close their eyes

with light, and walk home a hundred
and fifty bucks heavier. They don't know

their kids will be all right, as they brush noses, catch
the first startling whiff of the afterlife.

MEEROPOL

How strange, the *miracle* slant rhyme of your name,
a three syllable oasis, here in the White Pages

next to information I once knew by heart: the nape's
bouquet, the hip's cliff, the ear's hiding spot.

How simple it seemed that spring, with a quart of green
cactus milk between us, on the ferry from Naxos

to Crete, when the moon was the one clock, and stars
only had gums. And the summer in Barcelona

when the French children actually cried at the sight
of my dreadlocks. I used to think, if we kissed

in every time zone, it would always be the blue hour
in which I loved you. It still is. The literal

lightning bolt lodged in your family tree. The erased
surname. The alibi bone placed inside you.

A secret takes on a shape beyond language, becomes
tangible, something potentially broken

in half, for the world to see and give words to.

EXILE

Mathematicians still don't understand
the ball our hands made, or how

your electrocuted grandparents made it possible
for you to light my cigarettes with your eyes.

It isn't as simple as me climbing into the window
to leave six ounces of orange juice

and a doughnut by the bed, or me becoming
the sand you dug your toes in,

on the beach, when you wished
to hide them from the sun and the fixed eyes

of strangers, and your breath broke in waves
over my earlobe, splashing through my head, spilling out

over the opposite lobe, and my first poems
under your door in the unshaven light of dawn:

Your eyes remind me of a brick wall
about to hammered by a drunk
driver. I'm that driver. All night
I've swallowed you in the bar.

Once I kissed the scar, stretching its sealed
eyelid along your inner arm, dried

raining strands of hair, full of pheromones, discovered
all your idiosyncratic passageways, so I'd know

where to run when the cops came.
Your body is the country I'll never return to.

The man in charge of what crosses my mind
will lose fingernails for not turning you

away at the border. But at this moment
when sweat tingles from me, and

blame is as meaningless as shooting up a cow with milk,
I realize my kisses filled the halls of your body

with smoke, and the lies came
like a season. Most drunks don't die in accidents

they orchestrate, and I swallowed
a hand grenade that never stops exploding.

THREE

LAST NIGHT

There was a knock at one thirty-four.
The woman living above me
said she had to be up at six,
asked me to stop
thinking about my family.

I apologized, decided to clean
a week's worth of dishes in an hour.
As I scraped ketchup sludge
from the cracks in a plate,
a man across the street began yelling:

Put a sock in it, you
long-haired ding-dong,
You're waking up the neighborhood.
Your mother never loved you!

I closed the window,
poured a thick tongue of whiskey
over the silence of ice cubes
and shook the glass like a throat.

A wine bottle busted the window,
cradling the voice of an alley drunk:
You bullied your younger brothers,
you selfish schlock. Fill this up!

I kissed the bottle's lips,
lobbed it to the darkness, rearranged
my posters, changed my socks,
when there was a tap at the bedroom window.

The owner of the bar downstairs
crouched on the fire escape:
My customers can't hear the music, mac.
Here's a hundred bucks,
get a few drinks and a whore.

I grabbed him by the lobes and screamed,
listened to those tiny ear-bones rattle,
when the phone rang. It was the Mayor:

You missed your grandmother's birthday
again. Not even a phone call
after all she's given you.

That's it, I said, I'm leaving this city,
when a voice bullhorned:
This is the Chief of Police, son.

We know how you stole
your father's movie projector
and watched your older brother
take the rap for years.

I ran up the stairwell, hollering:
So what if I did!
Kicked open the roof door,
found my grandfather in his old chair.
He offered me a cigarette.

I never told your father I loved him.
Never kissed the sweat
from your grandmother's neck.
It's too late for me
but you got more time than a clock, boy.

Then he was gone.
I sat in the chair he left behind,
stared over the skulls of rooftops,
lonelier than the last tooth
in the mouth of a dead man.

1975

A son asks his father to spiral a football over a tree,
to arc it so the ball arrives an instant before the child.

The child dives–tendons extended, heart bucking, hands
opening jaw-like to clutch what descends from the sky:

Mother left today for the institution.
If the ball hits ground, she dies.

That December afternoon the boy's mother passed away
thirty-three times in the first hour.

Each time he grabbed her head from the snow
and ran it back to his father. Promised

to do better. And he did. He ran hard, focused, dove.
He caught Mother's skull thirteen times in a row

and she's still not coming home.

1976

The third grade teacher says: no homework
if this know-it-all can produce a future.

I can't find one in my knapsack.
Where is it? she asks. Did you leave it at home
with your mother?

Rodents of laughter scurry down the aisles.
She uses a finger to punctuate my chest.

Actually, my future's in a different time zone.
It ran off to Hollywood at an early age.

Hmpph! She tapes a sign to my desk:
FUTURELESS KNOW-IT-ALL and asks if I'm satisfied.
I'm not. I never will be.

During a lesson on natural disaster, her heart
beats her to death. I inform the class she swallowed
an earthquake and deposit
the FUTURELESS KNOW-IT-ALL sign in her hand.

I go outside, clutching only the present, and move
like time towards an open space.

1977

What are they waiting for?

The family around the table and a silence
so compact no words can break it.

Not even a pigeon swirling through the window
can nudge Mother's poorly taped grin.

Her face has the euphoric glow of a mathematician
whispering a formula into the whorl of a rose.

Her eyes are tiny stones testing the black
silk bags she lugs them in.

Since Father banned television the sons stare
at the marriage dangling from the ceiling.

Each month it sinks another couple inches
until it's in their food.

No wonder they don't eat.

WHERE THE SELF DIVIDES

I.

Loneliness is a privilege, and
I'm grateful for the afternoons I had as a child

to feed the crocodile I invented in my closet. How
the knob's wood expanded in my hand

when I threatened my best friend with death.
Twenty years later, he still has nightmares

where I get mad, fling open the door.
Downstairs our mothers were one mother,

measuring emptiness by the milligram. Their laughter
clung to the ceiling like balloons after a party.

Only they never came down. Stayed there
without color or reason. Bruises are genetic.

II.

By age ten we opened a window
and snapped our jaws at the world.

A flashlight's subtle patch on pavement
rendered bewilderment in nearly all who passed.

A bucket of water dumped from three stories up
onto the reliable shock of a stranger

made our hair electric, teeth sharp. Milk
bottles, barbells came next.

By twelve we slithered from the house's skin,
graffitied *crack, rom, rascal*

in the narrow throats of Philadelphia
and knocked over trash cans with our tails.

Under the dank wings of older kids on corners
we learned how to steal a chump's heart

without saying a word. By sixteen
anger's boomerang curved back at us.

There is a hole in the wall the size of a shield.
My fingers trace the hemline of a frenzy

passed down through the family
like an heirloom we can all squeeze into.

BAD SEEDS

Mother, you didn't need catastrophes.
Still, a soprano in your choir embraced them.

Chasing me under beds with a hymnal
when you already had the best hiding spots.

Thanks to the little blue things you planted
in your brain's blue field. Remember

sending me to the pharmacy to buy them?
I was eight when I found you lumped like a sack

of bad habits at the bottom of the staircase.
The numb smile. The donkey eyes.

I stood over the broken plate of your body.
Flicked donations across your irreversible lake.

I would've clutched the chorus that covered you
but I told you I couldn't be trusted.

GRANDFATHER

1908-1979

At sixteen on New Year's Eve, you swiped a cop car
and pumped out store windows
with a shotgun. Your uncle was town sheriff.

You liked westerns, poker, and building machines
in your basement, while spitting
emerald chunks into a wrinkled tissue.

In '74 doctors told you to choose between a nursing home
and a coffin. You stayed and kept banging
nails of smoke into the rice paper of your lungs.

You had three dreams: to own a house, a Cadillac,
and to ride in a Rolls Royce. Some nights
I want to dig you up and take you for that ride.

It was Christmas '79. We went to your house
like we always did. You gave presents like you always did.
We left before dusk like we never did.

The next day you cleaned your brains out with a shotgun
leaving behind a gray carpet with a red stain,
a melting widow, and no one to sit in your chair.

If only there were some secret telephone
I could drop in a coin and call you,
tell you about the life of your favorite grandson.

DEAD TWIN

This cup of skin is what our parents tilted,
poured that world into you: the survivor.

Your eyes are my hat, your thoughts my scarf.
Is it any wonder I'm coughing?

Any wonder puddles divide for my ankles?
I am the carrier of wet leaves.

What you forget to say.
Taking the words from your mouth

and listening.

FOUR

GRACE

Glance at a woman on a train platform.
Suddenly we've been married for years.

I know all the delicate nuances
in her nine dialects of silence.

Can pick her from a thousand others
just with a sniff of her neck.

We sit next to each other, as we always have.

Our elbows touch, like the tips of matches.
Exactly the way I remember.

When she says *excuse me, this is my stop,*
there is nothing awkward about it.

CHIVALRY

A woman asks to borrow my salt
but I know what she wants: me to juggle

goldfish around her bed while she dreams.

It's gonna take more than two buttons
unsnapped on that smile.

Please?

Who does she think she is, *pleasing*
for my salt in public?

I feel powerful, moral.

She folds up her sleeve, exposing
a tattoo of a goldfish.

No one sees. I nod.

She peels the bronze carp
from her bicep and swallows.

If you want salt, beg.

In the polished tusks of her calves
walking away, I see myself: transmogrified,

pure and glossy.

Hands pressed. Knees together.
I can't stand up.

KILL THE CARRIER

The sky is the color of a flamingo
trapped in an iceberg.

A three-legged dog charges towards me.

Despite the butter his head becomes
in my palm, he pants frantically.

He's run for weeks to tell me this.

I call the local canine expert.
She arrives at noon.

Since my immediate family died
in that bobsledding mishap

my holidays have been emptier
than the *o* in God.

I imagine spreading her thighs
over my toast,

us balancing an egg between our noses.

She says she must be alone
with the messenger.

Come back with the rain.

There is one small cloud in the so-called
corner of the sky.

It looks like the bagel with cream cheese
I've been dying to eat.

Why did she burst out laughing
at the portrait of my lone relative,

bald Uncle Vance, who I've never
located, let alone met?

There's one long cloud grilling
in the sky like a fish.

I remember a pub's ten-crown *pivo*
and the pretty Czech girls

marching in velvet stockings
the color of hope.

A herd of clouds stampedes across the sky.

Like a new lover, the sun's most beautiful
when coming or going.

Pour me a knuckle of moon over Prague, and I'll trickle
like blood from an executioner's ear.

Under a shattered windshield of stars

a paper boat hat, rocking on a drunk's head,
shoves off from its impossible harbor.

I return completely drenched.
All my cigarettes ruined.

There's a hairless man with his back to me
sitting on the floor.

A painting of that dog on the wall.

CRYPTOSPORIDIUM

Find meaning in this, and I'll slit a rabbit's throat
with the comma I keep between my teeth.
Nothing saves us.

The rug blooms with petals turning their backs on me.

My blood's a series of jumbled-up cubes and the cubes
mutate into triangles.

Were my parents legal the night they made me?

I am the pronouncer of side effects.

The triangles clang and the clanging would shatter
the windows in my temples, if temples had windows.

The more days I carry, the lighter they become.

After fifty-plus hours of sleeplessness
the external world adopts an early Goya glow.

I am a mood swinging between cities.

I hammer the clouds into place.

A bird-shaped balloon deflates
before flying away.

BEST INTENTIONS

From relentless hills of compromise, I peer
through borrowed binoculars

into the portholes of a rescue vessel: a nurse's sigh
floats on a patient's troubling aspects,

two elderly men hug and exchange labor camps,
a young man with enormous muscles openly sobs.

In the forest behind me, a gravedigger stands
by his shovel like commitment.

Beyond the trees, character assassins gather
in a warehouse brimming with toxic business cards.

Beyond that, madness dresses in a velour
confrontation, studded with bright metal threats.

A one-legged jogger, waving a forged permission slip,
rushes by and collapses on the brittle grass.

THE GOD HOLE

My vices race each other in a track meet.
The finish line is where eternity begins.

One false starts and takes an early lead
but can't shut up.

A second insults the others
because there's no corner to hide in.

Earth weeps a little faster.

A third pulls a bag of chips from his pocket
and munches away shamelessly.

Honey is the opposite of mustard.

A fourth nods her cloud at everything.

Another can't stop staring into the bleachers–
projecting his libido on random bad girl types.

In the sixth row a child beats his father
with a bottle of arthritis medicine.

A wound is a place insects return to.

When church bells are removed
the ears of Christ stop ringing.

OBJECTIVITY

There is a mob in the backyard
protesting my nightmare.

They wear t-shirts bearing the image
of the man who wants me dead.

They chant the same *Down with Jeff* slogan
so forcefully I swear it has a shadow.

What have I done to deserve this?
I pick up a sign and move among them

like a kind of silence murderers return to.
I join the chant against me and for the first time

a sense of belonging.